LYON TOWNSHIP LIBRARY
27005 MILFORD ROAD
P.O. BOX 326
NEW HUDSON, MICHIGAN

SMART STRUCTURES

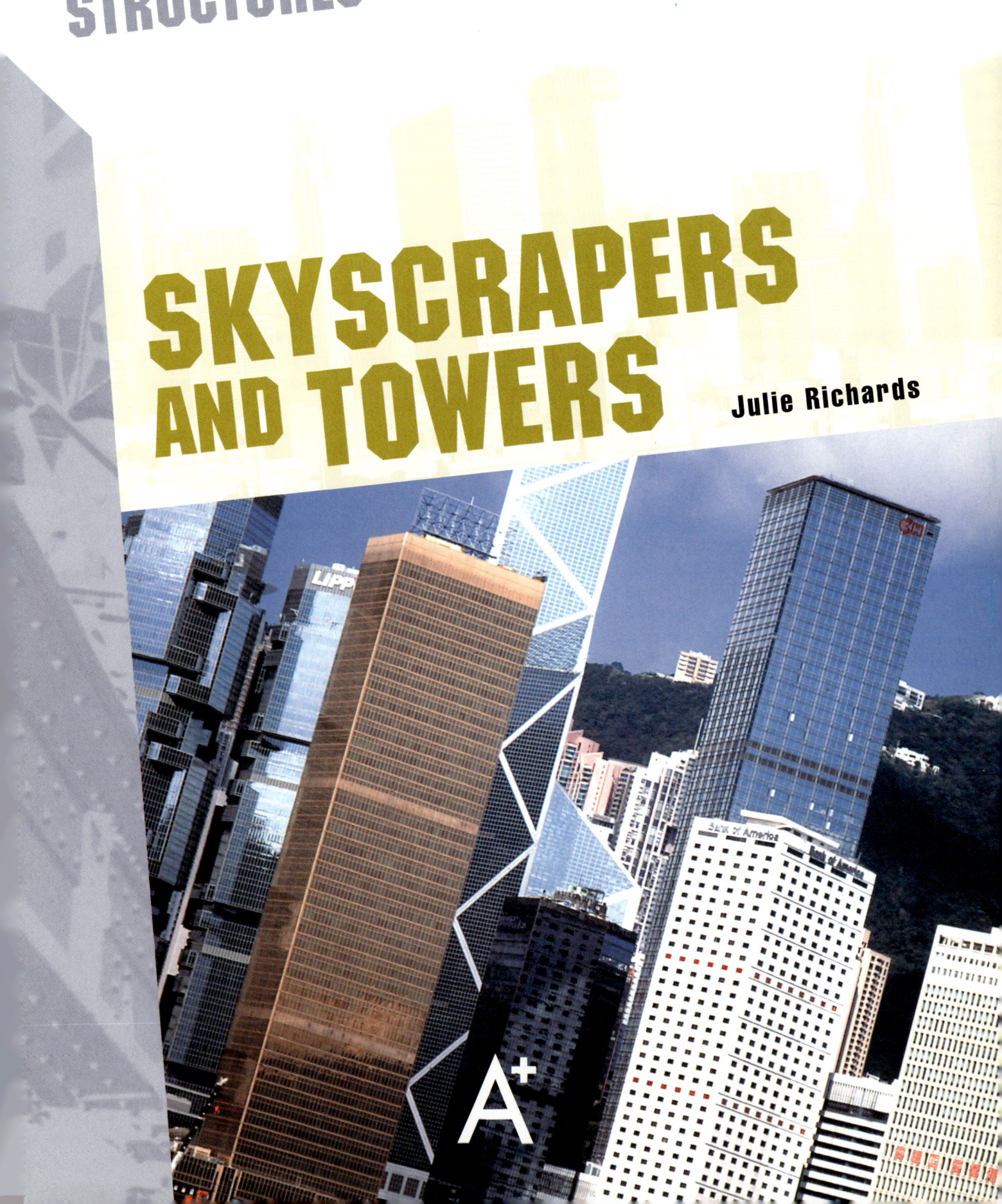

SKYSCRAPERS AND TOWERS

Julie Richards

This edition first published in 2004 in the United States of America by Smart Apple Media.

All rights reserved. No part of this book may be reproduced in any form or by any means without written permission from the publisher.

Smart Apple Media
1980 Lookout Drive
North Mankato
Minnesota 56003

Library of Congress Cataloging-in-Publication Data

Richards, Julie.
    Skyscrapers and towers / by Julie Richards.
       p. cm. — (Smart structures)
    Includes index.
    Summary: Describes different kinds of towers and skyscrapers, the methods and materials of their construction, and amazing or disastrous examples.
    ISBN 1-58340-348-5
    1. Towers—Design and construction—Juvenile literature. 2. Skyscrapers—Design and construction—Juvenile literature. [1. Towers—Design and construction. 2. Skyscrapers—Design and construction.] I. Title.
    TH2180.R53 2003
    720'.483—dc21   2002044613

First Edition
9 8 7 6 5 4 3 2 1

First published in 2003 by
MACMILLAN EDUCATION AUSTRALIA PTY LTD
627 Chapel Street, South Yarra, Australia 3141

Associated companies and representatives throughout the world.

Copyright © Julie Richards 2003

Edited by Anna Fern
Text design by Cristina Neri, Canary Graphic Design
Cover design by Cristina Neri, Canary Graphic Design
Layout by Nina Sanadze
Illustrations by Margaret Hastie, IKON Computergraphics
Photo research by Legend Images

Printed in Thailand

Acknowledgements
The author and the publisher are grateful to the following for permission to reproduce copyright material:

Cover photograph: Bank of China and other buildings, Hong Kong, courtesy of Getty Images.

AAP/AP Photo/Denis Poroy, p. 30; Australian Picture Library/Corbis, pp. 12, 15 (top), 17, 25; Getty Images, pp. 1, 5 (top, center bottom & bottom right), 7, 9, 10, 11, 18, 20 (bottom), 23, 24, 27, 28 (right), 29; © 2003 Mark A. Johnson, pp. 4, 16; Legend Images, pp. 15 (bottom), 28 (left); Photolibrary.com, p. 5 (left); Reuters, pp. 19, 20 (top), 21, 26.

While every care has been taken to trace and acknowledge copyright, the publisher tenders their apologies for any accidental infringement where copyright has proved untraceable. Where the attempt has been unsuccessful, the publisher welcomes information that would redress the situation.

CONTENTS

Skyscrapers and towers as structures 4

Looking at skyscrapers and towers 6
   Skyscraper shapes 6

The parts of a skyscraper 8

Building materials 10

Skyscraper and tower design 12
   Skyscraper design 13
   Tower design 15

Building skyscrapers 16
   Choosing the right design 16
   Foundations 17
   Putting up a steel frame 19
   Early skyscrapers 20
   Steel tubes 21
   Concrete frames 21
   Concrete columns 22
   Floors, walls, and services 23

Working skyscrapers 24
   Looking after skyscrapers 25

Skyscrapers that went wrong 26

Amazing skyscrapers and towers 28

Using models to learn about structures 30

Glossary 31

Index 32

KEY WORDS

When a word is printed in **bold** you can look up its meaning in the key words box on the same page. You can also look up the meaning of words in the glossary on page 31.

SKYSCRAPERS AND TOWERS AS STRUCTURES

A structure is made up of many different parts joined together. The shapes of the parts and the way they are joined together help a structure to stand up and do the job for which it has been designed. The **materials** used to make a structure can be made stronger or weaker, depending on their shape and how they are put together.

Skyscrapers and towers are made by humans, but there are also natural towers. People build skyscrapers and towers:

- to make better use of expensive building space on the ground
- to allow people to be close to work and to save traveling time
- to receive and transmit signals for telephones, radios, and television
- because they like the way they look.

KEY WORDS

structure something that is made up of many parts joined together

materials anything used to make a structure

Insects called termites made this natural tower by mixing soil with their saliva. This tower has many rooms connected by passages. It is waterproof and has places for fresh air to enter. It is like a living skyscraper filled with apartments. Other natural towers are made when water or wind rubs away rock over many thousands of years.

Types of skyscrapers

There are five types of skyscrapers made by humans:
- rigid frame
- braced frame
- **concrete** core
- steel-framed concrete core
- steel-framed tube.

The type of skyscraper built depends on what it is needed for and the place where it is to be built.

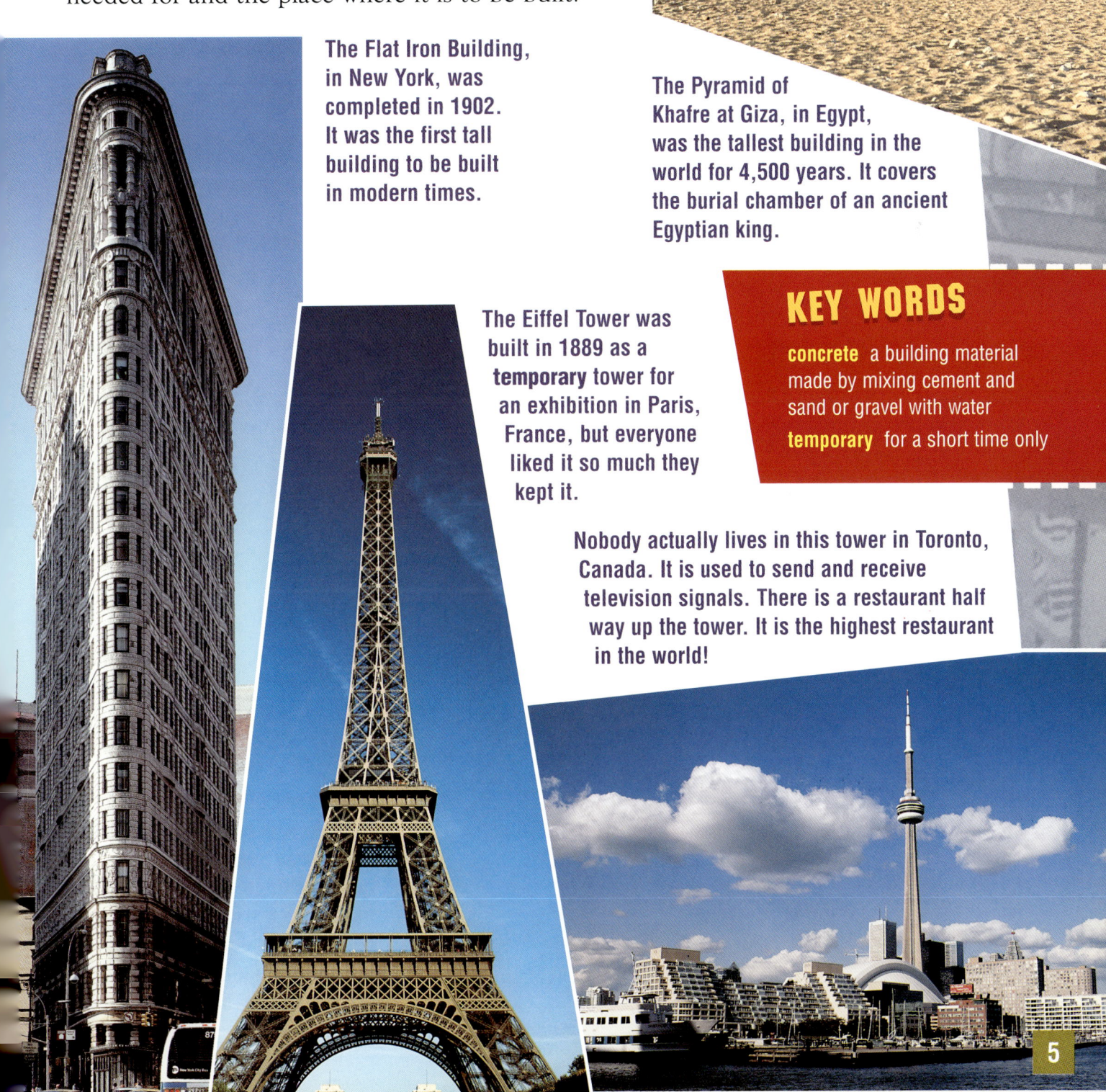

The Flat Iron Building, in New York, was completed in 1902. It was the first tall building to be built in modern times.

The Pyramid of Khafre at Giza, in Egypt, was the tallest building in the world for 4,500 years. It covers the burial chamber of an ancient Egyptian king.

The Eiffel Tower was built in 1889 as a **temporary** tower for an exhibition in Paris, France, but everyone liked it so much they kept it.

KEY WORDS

concrete a building material made by mixing cement and sand or gravel with water

temporary for a short time only

Nobody actually lives in this tower in Toronto, Canada. It is used to send and receive television signals. There is a restaurant half way up the tower. It is the highest restaurant in the world!

LOOKING AT SKYSCRAPERS AND TOWERS

If you look very closely at a skyscraper or tower, you will notice:
- the different parts which have been joined together to build it
- the shapes of these parts.

Skyscrapers must carry extremely heavy loads, such as the weight of their floors and walls, as well as the weight of the people and furniture inside them. Wind and earthquakes make a skyscraper or tower bend and shake. It is important that the different parts are made into the right shapes and joined together in the right way, or the skyscraper or tower will not be safe.

Skyscraper shapes

Some shapes are stronger than others, but they all have their breaking point. Rectangles and triangles are two of the strongest shapes and are used to build skyscrapers and towers.

Rectangle

One elephant on a rectangle makes the top side bend. The weight of three elephants causes the top side to break.

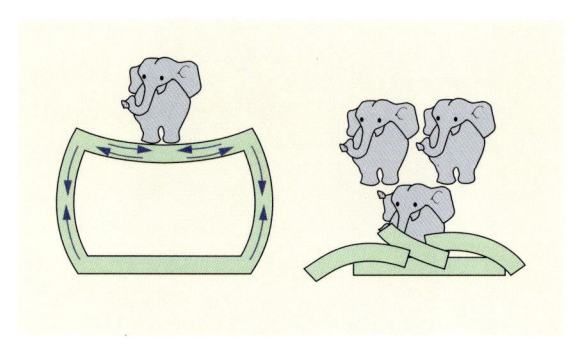

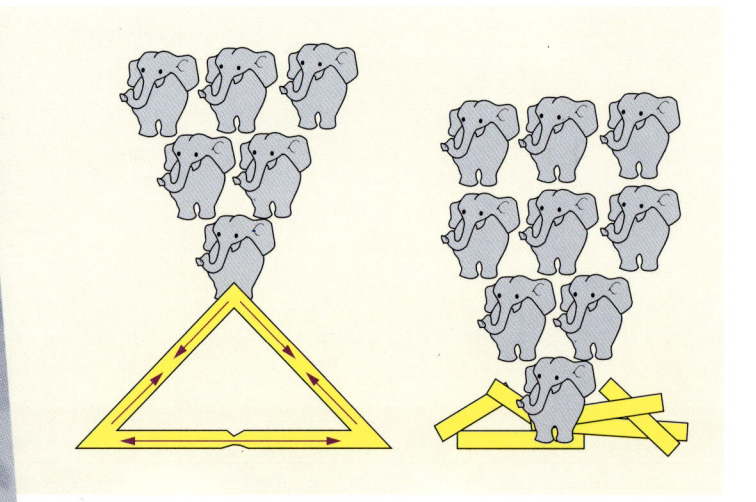

Triangle

The weight of six elephants on a triangle causes the two top sides to squeeze together and the bottom side to pull apart. The triangle is the strongest shape, but a herd of elephants makes the bottom side stretch so much that it snaps in half.

Can weaker shapes be made stronger?

Rectangles are not as strong as triangles. Rectangles can be made stronger by using extra pieces of building material to make them into triangles. An extra piece like this is called a **brace**.

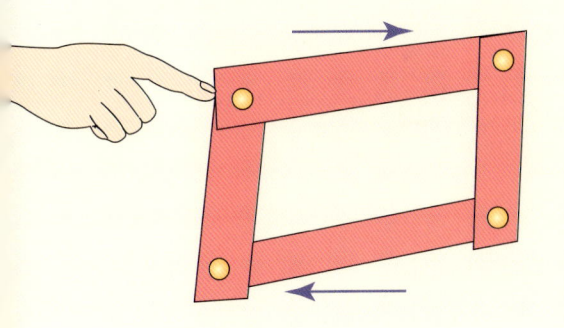

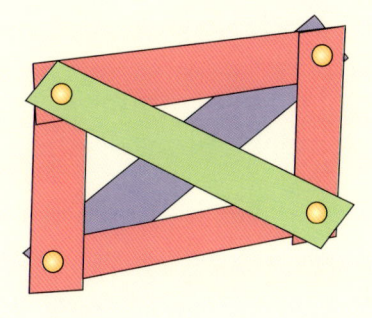

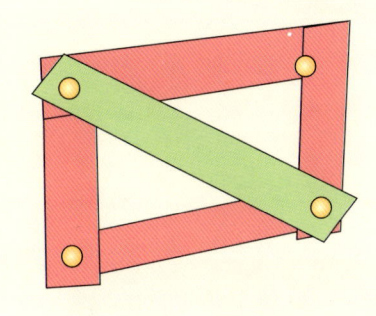

The sides of a rectangle are weak and can be easily moved about.

Fixing two pieces of material to a rectangle makes it stiffer and stronger.

One of the extra pieces can be taken away without weakening the rectangle.

Triangles

Triangles are the strongest, stiffest, and most **stable** of all the shapes. You can see the triangles in the framework of tall structures such as cranes and electricity towers. Some of these triangles are made from rectangles which have been braced.

KEY WORDS

brace something fastened to an object to keep it stiff and straight, just like the braces worn on teeth

stable something that will not wobble or fall

When a giraffe bends over to drink, its long neck makes it very unstable. So the giraffe spreads its front legs to make a strong, stable triangle.

Pyramids

You may have watched people building a human pyramid. They can get quite high and still not collapse. Do you think that the same number of people could make a tower just as high by standing on each other's shoulders? Would it be as stable as the pyramid? No, it would not. The pyramid is a type of triangle that supports the weight at its top by spreading the load through its wide base.

THE PARTS OF A SKYSCRAPER

All skyscrapers have **foundations**, a framework, and walls. Without these important parts, a skyscraper cannot do the job for which it has been designed.

KEY WORDS

foundations a firm base upon which a structure is built

Foundations

The foundations of a tall building are like feet, because the building uses them to stand up. These feet go deep into the ground and stop the building from toppling over in the wind, falling over during an earthquake, or sinking under its own weight. Most foundations are holes filled with concrete and super-strong metal. Tall buildings sway and shake a little when strong winds blow or the ground around them moves. The foundations soak up the shaking, just like a sponge.

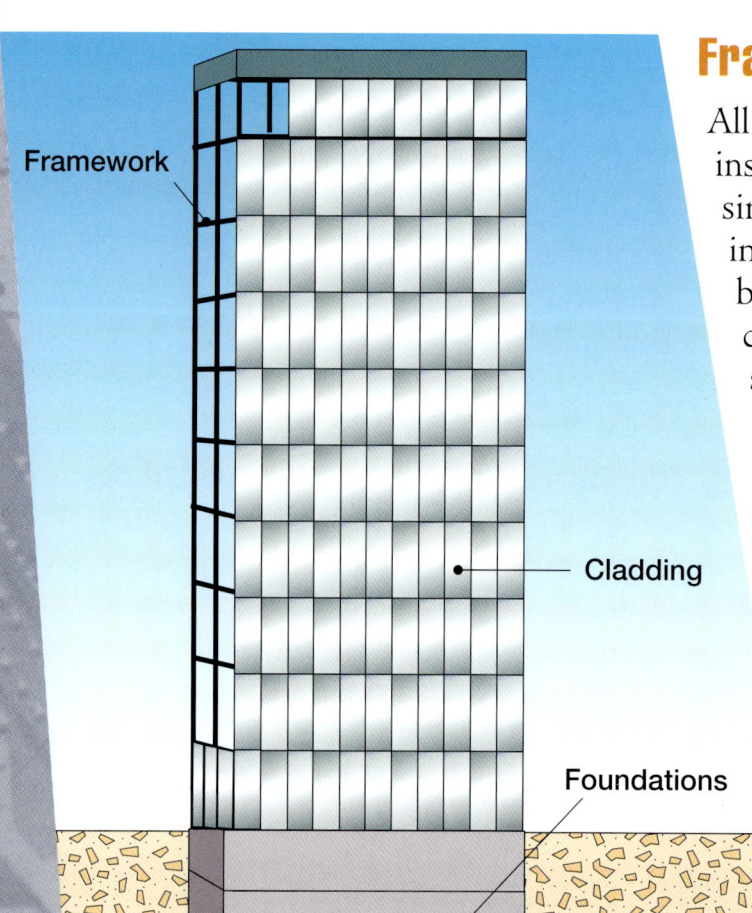

Framework

All skyscrapers have a framework inside them. The framework does a similar job to the bony skeleton inside your body. It holds the building up and stops it from collapsing. Most modern skyscrapers have a solid column in the middle of the skeleton, just like a human spine.

Cladding

The windows and walls are like a skin covering the skeleton of a skyscraper. They are mostly made of glass, plastic panels, or thin sheets of stone or concrete. The skin of a skyscraper is called cladding.

Allowing for movement

A skyscraper must be **flexible**. A tower that has an open frame, such as a tower carrying overhead powerlines, allows the wind to blow straight through the structure, which lessens any shaking or swaying. Skyscrapers are stiff, solid structures. The wind hits the building and flows around it. The force of a strong wind hitting a building causes it to sway. Some skyscrapers can sway 6 to 10 feet (2–3 m).

Engineers design tall buildings so that they can move with the wind, just as a tree does. If a tree did not sway, its trunk would snap or its branches could be torn away.

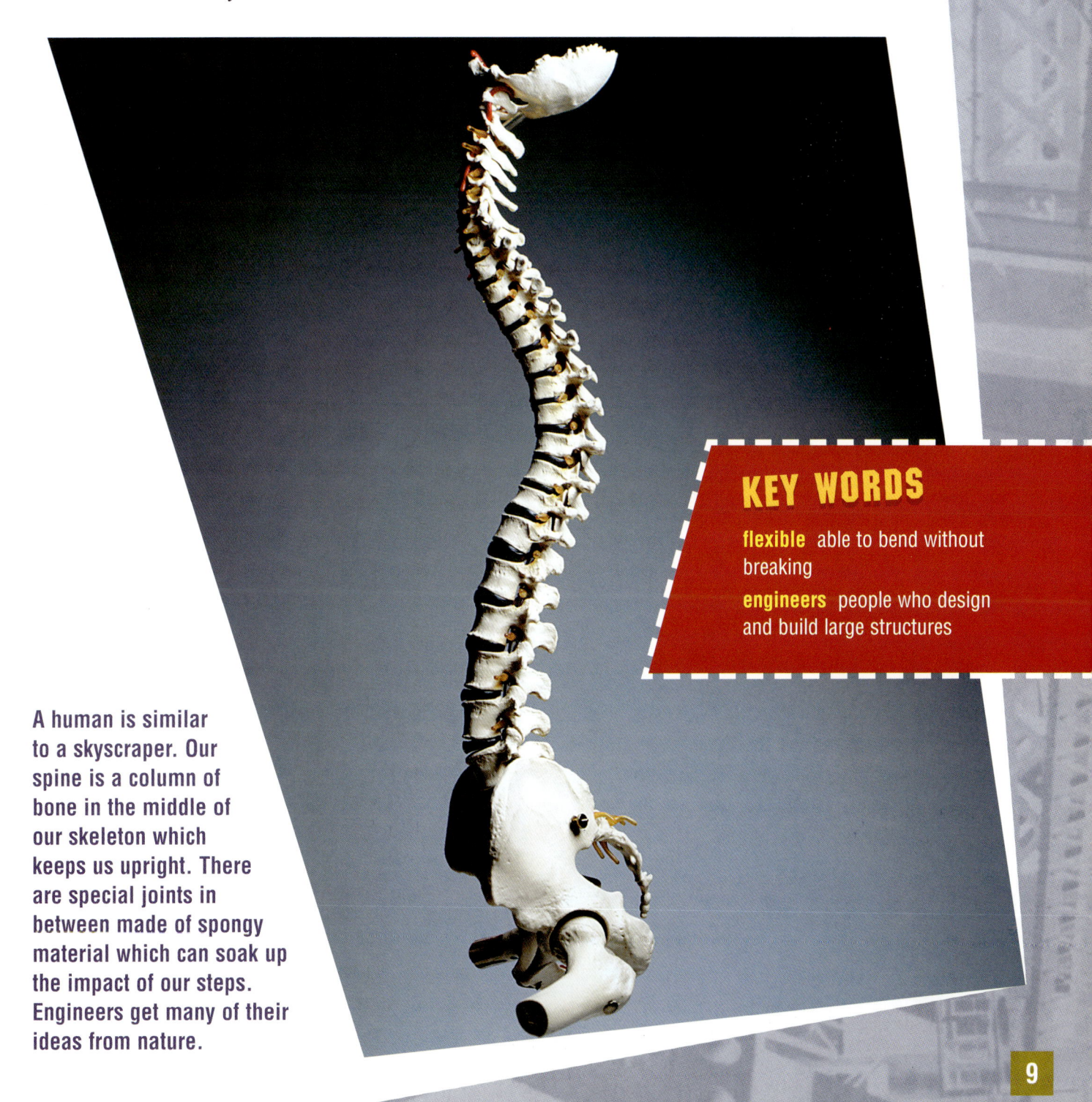

KEY WORDS

flexible able to bend without breaking

engineers people who design and build large structures

A human is similar to a skyscraper. Our spine is a column of bone in the middle of our skeleton which keeps us upright. There are special joints in between made of spongy material which can soak up the impact of our steps. Engineers get many of their ideas from nature.

BUILDING MATERIALS

Early skyscrapers were made of very heavy materials such as iron and stone. They could not be built very high because the foundations could not support the weight of the building. Tall towers were often little more than an iron skeleton. Without walls, floors, objects, and people to support, they carried little extra weight and could be built much higher.

Eiffel Tower

The Eiffel Tower was completed by Gustave Eiffel in 1889 for the Paris World Fair. It was the first tall structure to be made from iron. One hundred iron workers made the 18,038 individual pieces and 121 men assembled them at the site. The pieces were joined together by hot **rivets**. It took a team of four men to fix each of the 2,500,000 rivets used: one to heat it, another to hold it in place, a third to shape the rivet's top or head, and a fourth to beat it with a sledgehammer. As the rivets cooled, they shrank, ensuring the pieces were held together as tightly as possible.

The first part of the tower was built using wooden scaffolding 131 feet (40 m) high. As the tower grew higher, the pieces were hauled up by steam-powered cranes, which climbed the tower as they went. Until the Empire State Building was built, in 1931, the Eiffel Tower was the tallest human-made structure in the world, measuring 984 feet (300 m) high.

> **KEY WORDS**
> **rivets** pins which are used to fasten sheets of metal together

◀ It took two years to build the Eiffel Tower. Here it is under construction.

Steel

Today, most skyscrapers are made of steel and concrete. Steel is made mostly of iron, but it is much lighter, stronger, and more flexible. Steel is used to make the skyscraper frame. A steel cable as thick as your finger could lift a 33-ton (30-t) truck without snapping!

Members

A skyscraper frame is made up of **vertical** pieces, called columns, and **horizontal** pieces, called beams. Each column or beam is called a member. The ends of the beams look like the letters I or H. Beams this shape are much stronger and lighter than square beams. The columns support the ends of the beams, and the beams support the floors. The columns on each floor support the weight of all the floors above. So, the columns at the bottom have to be the strongest columns of all. The frame itself is very heavy.

> Designers can make the frame a part of the look of the skyscraper's design. You can see the triangular braces on the Bank of China building, in Hong Kong (the tallest building in the photo).

Concrete

Concrete is a mixture of **cement**, water, sand, and gravel. The wet, runny mixture dries to become strong and hard as rock. Concrete is so strong that you could stand a 33-ton (30-t) truck on a mug-sized chunk without crushing it into crumbs. However, concrete cracks quite easily when it is stretched. Steel is able to be stretched. Pouring wet concrete over flexible steel bars strengthens the concrete and stops it from cracking as it stretches. Flexible steel bars are added to any part of a structure that will be stretched. This is called **reinforced** concrete.

Cladding materials

The framework of the building is covered by cladding materials which are light and strong, weatherproof and attractive. They include light metals such as stainless steel and aluminum, glass, brick, and stone. Glass is specially coated to stop too much of the sun's heat from getting into the building. Only metals that resist rusting are used, and the brick and stone are cut into thin slices to make them lighter.

KEY WORDS

vertical standing upright
horizontal level or flat
cement an ingredient in concrete which makes the concrete harden like stone
reinforced made stronger

SKYSCRAPER AND TOWER DESIGN

Engineers do a lot of research to make sure the right type of skyscraper or tower is designed. Science has helped engineers to find out about stronger, more stable designs, lighter building materials, and new tools that do the job faster. Engineers use many of the shapes or structures that are seen in nature. New technologies such as steel and reinforced concrete have allowed skyscrapers to be built even higher. Computers can create "walk-through" models that show the inside of a building as if you are walking through it. Scientists use a **wind tunnel** to test a model of the structure so that they can see how the wind might affect it.

The John Hancock Center, in Chicago, was designed to withstand very high winds. The building is narrower at the top and its walls are strengthened by crossed metal braces.

The Sears Tower, in Chicago, is 1,453 feet (443 m) high. Although it was completed in 1973, it is still the second tallest building in the world (Petronas Towers in Malaysia are the tallest). Modern design and new technologies would allow a building at least 3,282 feet (1,000 m) high to be built, but nobody has built one. Why? To build that high would be too expensive. Another reason is that an extremely tall building would sway so much in the wind that the people inside it would feel sick.

KEY WORDS

wind tunnel a specially built tunnel where fans are used to move the air at different speeds

Skyscraper design

Not all skyscrapers are built in the same way. Engineers and **architects** often combine ideas and designs to suit the special conditions in the area where the skyscraper is to be built. There are five basic designs that they can use:

- rigid-frame structure
- braced-frame structure
- concrete core
- steel-framed concrete core
- steel-framed tube.

Rigid-frame design

A rigid-frame structure is made up of columns and connecting beams. Each part of the structure carries some of the weight, including the walls. The first skyscrapers were built this way.

Braced-frame design

A braced-frame structure is like a rigid-frame structure, but it has bracing added to make it more stable. This design is suitable for areas that experience strong winds or earthquakes, because the bracing helps to reduce side-to-side swaying. Skyscrapers built this way can be taller and stronger than rigid-frame skyscrapers.

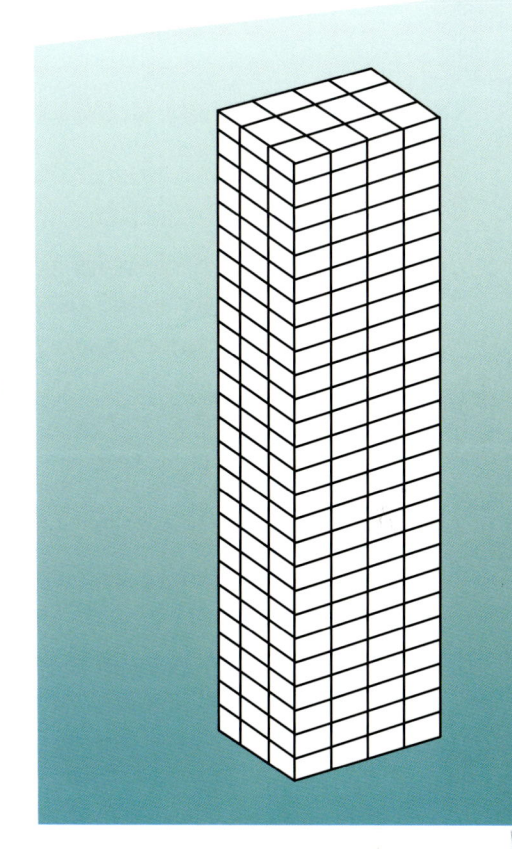

▲ A rigid-frame design

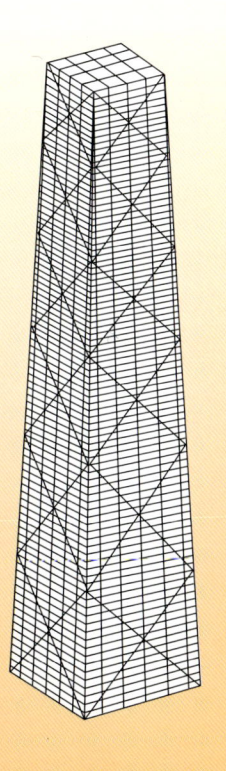

◀ A braced-frame design

KEY WORDS

architects people who design buildings

SKYSCRAPER AND TOWER DESIGN

Concrete-core design

A concrete-core design has a central core made of concrete. Columns branch out from the core to support the floors, like branches sprouting from a tree trunk. The walls do not carry any weight. This type of skyscraper is strong enough for buildings about 40 stories high in an area where there are no earthquakes.

Steel-framed concrete-core design

A steel-framed concrete-core design has a steel frame as well as the central concrete column. The central core and the steel frame work together to help prevent the building from swaying in strong winds.

▲ A concrete-core design

A steel-framed tube design ▶

Steel-framed tube design

A steel-framed tube skyscraper is the strongest structure. This design allows skyscrapers to be more than 100 stories high. A steel-framed tube structure is made of steel beams, which are joined to each other to form hollow tubes. The walls and floors are attached to the steel-framed tubes. The steel tubes can also be joined together in bundles to make an even stronger and taller structure.

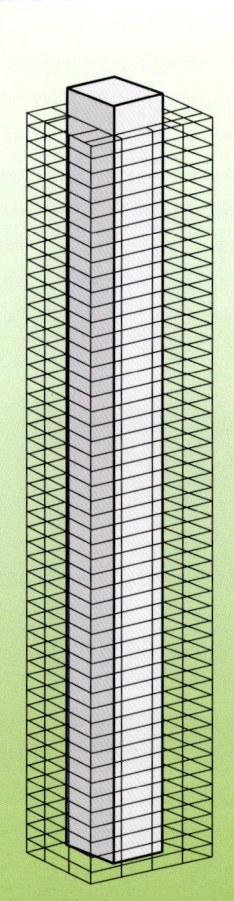

◀ You can see the central concrete-core design that supports the steel frame in this building.

Tower design

Towers can be very simple structures with only one purpose. Electricity towers, for example, carry dangerous high-voltage electricity from a power station to where it is needed. Towers like these are the safest and cheapest way to carry electricity over long distances. They stand on strong legs anchored in concrete slabs to make them stable and, like towers such as the Eiffel Tower, do not have a skin covering their skeleton.

The Eiffel Tower became a radio antenna and carried the first radio time signal across the Atlantic Ocean to Canada in 1910. These signals enabled sailors to measure time and distance more accurately so they did not become lost at sea.

A watchtower is placed on top of a hill in an area of thick forest so that fire spotters see smoke before a wildfire gets too close. The fire spotters sit in the cabin. They use a radio to tell fire fighters about the position and size of the fire, and how fast it is moving.

Guyed tower

A guyed tower is supported by steel cables that pull on the tower from different directions. The cables all pull with the same amount of strength, so the pulling force is balanced and the tower remains upright. Think about a tug-of-war. What happens when two tug-of-war teams pull with the same amount of strength? They stay still because their pulling forces balance each other. A guyed tower works in the same way.

The 1,000-foot-high (305-m) Centrepoint Tower, in Sydney, Australia, is a guyed tower supported by 56 steel cables. If laid end to end, these cables would stretch from Sydney to New Zealand.

BUILDING SKYSCRAPERS

Building a skyscraper is an enormous job which can take hundreds of workers several years to finish.

Choosing the right design

Choosing a design for a new skyscraper depends on what the building is to be used for and where it is to be built. **Geologists** test samples of rock and soil in a laboratory to discover if there are any weaknesses in the ground. Engineers can then decide which type of foundations are needed and how deep they should be. The engineers also work out how much the building will weigh, how much extra weight it will carry when it has people and furniture inside it, and how much it will move when the wind blows.

KEY WORDS

geologists scientists who study rocks and soil

Special shapes

The shape of a building can be very important. The Trans-America Building, in San Francisco, was built like a pyramid to withstand earthquakes. The weight of its 61 floors is supported on a wide base, with lots of braced rectangles for extra strength. Being wide at the bottom and narrow at the top means that it will not topple over when the ground shakes.

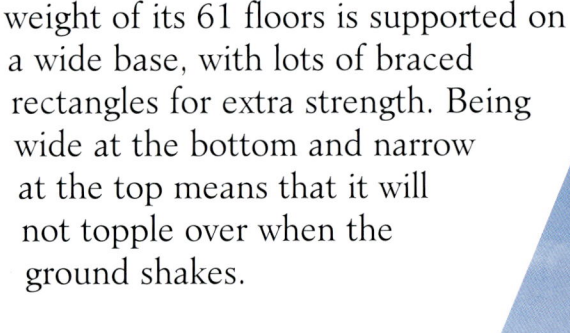

The Trans-America Building, in San Francisco (the highest building in the photo) ▶

Foundations

Have you ever stood on the beach and felt yourself sink into the sand? The heavier you are, the deeper you sink. Just imagine how far you would sink if 100 people stood on your shoulders. If you were standing on solid rock, you would not sink at all. The best place to build a skyscraper is on the solid rock, called bedrock, that forms part of Earth's crust.

Protecting nearby buildings

All foundations require very deep holes. Digging such deep holes can make the foundations of nearby buildings move, so a thick wall is built around the inside of the hole to stop the soil from slipping into it. The holes are dug by **excavators** and the soil from the holes is taken away by dump trucks.

Solid rock

Many of New York's skyscrapers stand on **piles** made of steel or reinforced concrete. Piles act like the roots of a tree and stop the skyscraper from blowing over or sinking. A tool like a giant **corkscrew** twists its way into the ground until it reaches solid rock. A steel rod is put into the hole, and concrete is poured around it. Sometimes an enormous hammer, called a pile-driver, is lifted up by a crane and then dropped onto the pile until it is buried deep enough in the ground.

> **KEY WORDS**
>
> **excavators** people or machines that dig
>
> **piles** concrete or metal poles buried in the ground
>
> **corkscrew** spiral-shaped or spinning like a spiral

Constructing the foundations of the Great Wall Hotel in Beijing, China ▼

BUILDING SKYSCRAPERS

Soft ground

Soft ground has no bedrock and cannot support piles. Instead, a concrete slab called a raft is poured. The raft is much wider than the area the building will stand on, so the weight will be spread out through the slab. A concrete raft works very much like a raft used on water. If you try and sit on the surface of water, you sink because you are too heavy. But you can sit on a raft without sinking. This is because the weight of your body is spread evenly through the raft, making it easier to support. A concrete slab beneath a skyscraper does the same thing.

Luckily, skyscrapers weigh much less than they once did. Stone, bricks, and iron have been replaced by much lighter materials, such as aluminum. The less a skyscraper weighs, the less support it will need. This makes it cheaper and faster to build.

Leaning Tower of Pisa

The Leaning Tower of Pisa, in Italy, is built on soft, wet ground. Even before the tower was finished, 800 years ago, it began to tilt as its foundations sank beneath its weight. The tilt became so dangerous that the tower was close to collapsing. Since 1999, engineers have been working to make the tower safe for tourists, finishing most of the work in 2001. By using 41 corkscrew drills especially designed for the job, engineers have slowly removed 33 tons (30 t) of soil from beneath one side of the tower. As the tower gently sank into the new cavity, it began to straighten itself. Steel cables were attached to the tower to support it while the soil was removed.

◀ **The Leaning Tower of Pisa shows what happens when a structure is not built on firm foundations.**

Putting up a steel frame

The bottom sections of the frame are fixed to the foundations so that the frame cannot move about or fall over. The rest of the frame is made up of flat pieces of steel which are **welded** together at a factory. They are delivered to the site and put together like a giant construction kit. Huge tower cranes lift the pieces into position. The cranes are built on site bit by bit, getting taller as the building grows. Tower cranes can be as high as 15 houses piled on top of one another. Other, shorter cranes are fixed to the frame farther up, so that they can reach the highest floors.

Cranes are fixed to the frame of this skyscraper to reach the highest floors. ▼

A giant construction kit

Each piece of the frame is numbered so that everyone knows where it goes. All the pieces are sprayed with a special fireproof coating. Some pieces have holes drilled in them, ready to be bolted to the other pieces with special steel pins called rivets. The rivets are punched through the holes and their ends flattened to stop them from slipping out again. The parts of the frame which must be joined end to end are welded together for added strength.

The workers are attached to the building by safety harnesses. They wear hard hats to protect their heads from being side-swiped by swinging beams or hit by falling tools.

KEY WORDS

welded two pieces of metal joined together by heating their ends until they melt into one

BUILDING SKYSCRAPERS

Concrete columns

When some skyscrapers are built, the first part to be erected is a huge concrete column. This reinforced concrete core is the spine of the skyscraper that holds it upright. A concrete core is built using formwork. Concrete is poured into the formwork. As the concrete sets, more layers are added and the concrete core slowly grows taller. Fresh, runny concrete in huge buckets is lifted by cranes or pumped through thick hoses. **Hoists** are fixed to the outside of the scaffolding to carry workers and materials higher up the column as it grows. Concrete beams that will support each floor spread out from the column like branches from the trunk of a tree.

Some frames are just like a tree. They have a deep root and floors branching out from a trunk.

More space

A central core creates more space inside a building because there is no need to place supporting columns around the floor. The space inside the core is useful as an elevator shaft, or for running pipes, wires, and cables between floors.

Engineers have borrowed some of their ideas from looking at termite colonies. A termite colony has a central core, too. Its core is made of clay and supports the ceiling and most of the nest. The core also runs several feet below ground, acting as a foundation. Extra shafts are dug below the core as part of an air-conditioning system. The difference between human designers and termites is that teams of blind termite workers build a termite skyscraper in total darkness.

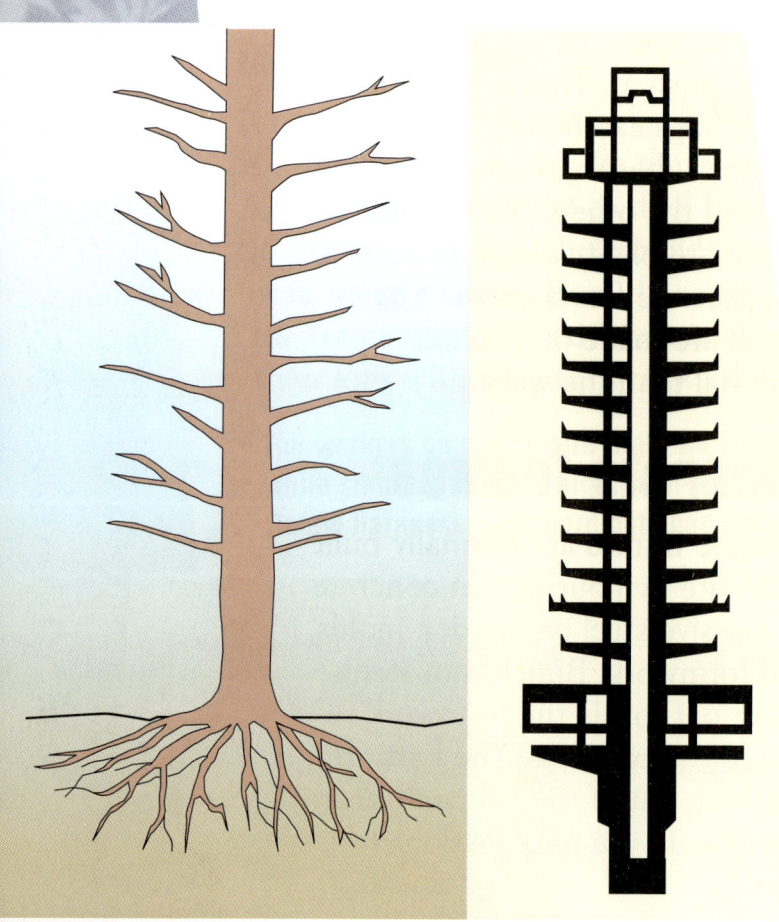

KEY WORDS

hoists machines specially made for lifting very heavy things

Floors, walls, and services

As the frame for each floor of the skyscraper is finished, work begins on the floor itself. The walls are also added, making the floors below waterproof. Services such as electricity, water pipes, air-conditioning, and telephone cables are installed.

Floors and walls

Depending on the design of the building, the floors will be hung from a central core or fixed to the main steel or concrete framework. Floors are made by pouring concrete onto corrugated steel plates. The plates are stacked in the order they will be needed and hoisted up to the right height, as required. The walls are added in sections and attached to the outside of the frame. The cladding might be thin sheets of metal or enormous panes of glass. Narrow strips of rubber are placed between the sections of cladding to stop water from leaking through.

This steel floor deck is being concreted. The long hose is a concrete pump. The builders are smoothing out the poured concrete.

Services

Before anyone can live or work in a skyscraper, workers must install services such as electricity, water tanks and pipes, telephones, air-conditioning, elevators, washrooms, and waste-disposal chutes. Hundreds of miles of wiring, pipes, ducts, and cables are needed to connect everything together. These are fitted under each floor and hidden when the ceiling panels are added. Inside walls are installed to divide the floors into rooms or offices. When the carpets are laid and the final decorations finished, the skyscraper will be ready for its first occupants.

WORKING SKYSCRAPERS

There can be as many people living and working in a big skyscraper as there are in a small town. Computers control the skyscraper's temperature, telephone systems, elevators, electricity supply, and fire alarms. The computer can even make the building move when necessary!

When the wind blows

Most skyscraper frames are welded and bolted so the whole structure moves like a swaying tree trunk rather than twisting against itself. The Citicorp Center, in New York, was the first building to use a tuned mass damper (T.M.D.) to help balance the building on windy days. The T.M.D. is a 433-ton (393-t) concrete block at the top of the skyscraper, which is pushed from one side of the building to the other on rollers. When the building sways in one direction, the block rolls across in the other direction. The extra weight pulls the building with it in the same way that you might balance a see-saw.

Thousands of people can move in and out of just one skyscraper in a day. Computers control all the systems that make the building comfortable and keep people safe.

When the ground shakes

Earthquakes can strike without warning. Some buildings have rubber pads or springs at their base to absorb the shaking. The San Francisco Airport, in California, has a giant steel **ball bearing** beneath each of its 267 supporting columns. Each ball rests in a bowl-shaped base that is connected to the ground. When the ground shakes, the ball bearing rolls around in its base, soaking up most of the movement and protecting the building from violent shaking.

KEY WORDS

ball bearing a metal ball placed between two things to allow them to move smoothly against each other

Going up and down

The first elevators in tall buildings were operated by steam-powered engines. Modern elevators are pulled up and down shafts on massive cables that are run by electric motors. Special emergency brakes can stop the elevator if the power fails or one of the cables snaps. Some elevators stop at all floors, while express elevators go straight to the upper floors. The elevators in the John Hancock Center in Chicago travel at 1,801 feet (549 m) per minute—nearly three floors every second!

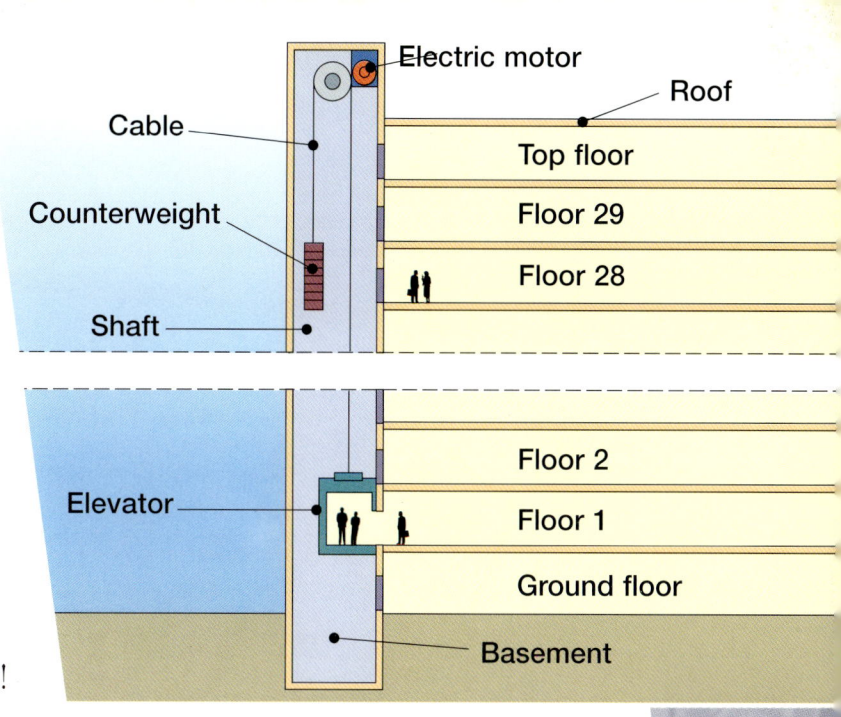

An elevator moves up and down in a shaft and is hung on a cable powered by an electric motor.

Keeping cool

All skyscrapers have to be air-conditioned to keep the people inside them comfortable because the windows are never opened. Glass walls make the sun's rays more powerful, so keeping the skyscraper cool is more of a problem than keeping it warm. The air-conditioning equipment on the roof of the skyscraper draws in fresh air and sends it around the building through large pipes, called ducts. Most skyscrapers have revolving doors on the ground floor. These doors help keep the temperature steady. If these buildings had rows of sliding doors that kept opening and closing, these would let the wind blast in.

Looking after skyscrapers

The people who look after skyscrapers and towers do a very important job. They make sure that the elevators, telephones, air-conditioning, electricity, gas, and water supplies are always working. Safety equipment such as fire alarms, smoke detectors, and sprinklers must also be kept working properly in case there is an emergency.

Engineers use ropes to climb the building to check and repair any part of the outside structure that is leaking or which has become loose and is in danger of falling onto the people below. Window cleaners work from a cradle which moves along the building on a special cable. It can take many weeks to clean all of the windows of a skyscraper. When the cleaners finish the last window, it is usually time to start again.

Some modern skyscrapers have their elevators, pipes, and cables on the outside of the building.

SKYSCRAPERS THAT WENT WRONG

Most modern skyscrapers are built to carry heavy loads of people and equipment without falling over or sinking into the ground. They are also designed to withstand earthquakes and high winds. When disaster does strike, it is often in a poorer country.

Different countries

When an earthquake struck San Francisco in 1989, it killed 65 people and damaged only a few buildings. An earthquake of the same strength happened in the less wealthy country of Armenia some months earlier. In 30 seconds, it killed 100,000 people and wiped out nearly all the buildings in two of Armenia's major cities.

Not all countries in the world can afford to buy strong building materials. They do not have enough experts with the special equipment or knowledge needed to design and build earthquake-proof structures. Often these people are so poor that they have little choice but to live in very crowded and unsafe housing. In wealthier countries, special building laws are made to ensure that everyone is as safe as possible.

◀ This apartment block collapsed during an earthquake because the concrete frame was not strong enough.

The Citicorp Center

Even in a wealthy country, a mistake can happen. The chief engineer of the Citicorp Center in New York discovered that the bolted joints in the skyscraper's frame were too weak to withstand a hurricane wind. A team of welders spent three months welding two-inch-thick (50-mm) steel plates over each of the building's 200 bolted joints. Six weeks into the repairs, a major hurricane was heading for the area. Luckily, the hurricane swung away, out to sea.

Unusual events

A well designed and properly built skyscraper can be one of the safest places to be, but sometimes an unexpected event can destroy even the strongest building.

The Empire State Building

In 1945, during heavy **fog**, a huge B-25 bomber aircraft flew straight into the 78th floor of the Empire State Building. Several people, including the aircraft's crew, were killed. The building's sturdy steel frame survived the collision.

> **KEY WORDS**
>
> **fog** a thick mist of water droplets that hangs in the air

The Empire State Building's heavy steel frame with its stone panels withstood the force of an aircraft crashing into it. ▶

World Trade Center

On September 11, 2001, both towers of the World Trade Center, New York, collapsed after terrorists crashed two hijacked aircraft into them. This taught engineers an important lesson about how much a skyscraper frame can handle. Both towers were a steel-tube design and easily withstood the force of the collisions. However, terrible fires, which had been started by burning aircraft fuel, destroyed the fireproof coating on the steel frames. The steel became so hot that it began to stretch like melted cheese. That much stretching made the frames too thin and weak, causing part of each tower to collapse under the weight of the concrete floors above.

AMAZING SKYSCRAPERS AND TOWERS

There are some very tall structures which you may not think of as skyscrapers or towers, but they are.

Skyscrapers at sea

An oil rig may not look very tall because all you see above the water is the platform. If the sea was drained away, you would see that some oil rigs stand on immense concrete legs driven down into the sea-bed. Others are anchored to the sea-bed by thick steel cables. Just like a skyscraper, an oil rig has offices, rooms where workers live, entertainment areas, and a place for helicopters to land. The tower houses the huge drill that digs its way down to the oil. Oil and gas is pumped up through the pipes inside the legs to be separated and cleaned. The tower on top of the oil rig is called a derrick. It holds the drill. Some oil rigs are taller than the Empire State Building.

▲ An oil rig can be as tall as a skyscraper.

Lighthouses

A lighthouse is a slim tower with a light at the top to show ships at sea that they may be close to dangerous rocks and reefs. The world's first lighthouse was built in ancient Egypt in 270 B.C. It was 400 feet (122 m) high. The light was a fire, which had to be kept burning all through the night. Modern lighthouses have a computer which switches an electric light on and off. Many lighthouse lights are powered by the sun's energy.

Early weapons used round balls of lead, called shot, which were made in a shot tower. Lead was melted and poured through the holes in a net at the top of the tower. As the lead dropped, the air smoothed it into a round ball. Each ball would drop into a large container of water at the bottom to be cooled.

Skyscraper facts and firsts

Many of the world's most amazing structures are skyscrapers and towers. Some are record-breakers because of their height. Other skyscrapers and towers are famous because they were the first to use certain building materials or because ways of solving difficult problems were found during their building. Here are some interesting facts and figures—there are many more you can find out about.

The world's highest skyscraper

The Petronas Towers, in Kuala Lumpur, Malaysia, is the tallest building in the world. Soaring 1,483 feet (452 m) above the city, the towers are joined 41 floors above the ground by the world's highest skybridge. It takes 90 seconds to travel from the underground car park to the top of each tower. The steel used in the towers weighs more than 3,000 elephants! Together, the towers have 32,000 windows. It takes window washers a month to wash each tower just once.

Petronas Towers ▶

Canada National Tower

The tallest free-standing structure in the world is not a skyscraper, but a tower. The 1,815-foot-tall (553-m) Canada National Tower is as high as five playing fields stacked on top of one another and weighs the same as 23,214 adult elephants. A Russian Sikorsky helicopter flew into the city to lift the 44 pieces of television antenna into place on top of the tower. The tower opened in 1976. The tower's world records include having the world's longest metal staircase and the world's highest wine cellar.

Petronas Towers is the tallest building because its spires are included in its structure. The Sears Tower antennas were added later and are not part of the building. The CN Tower's antenna is not part of the building.

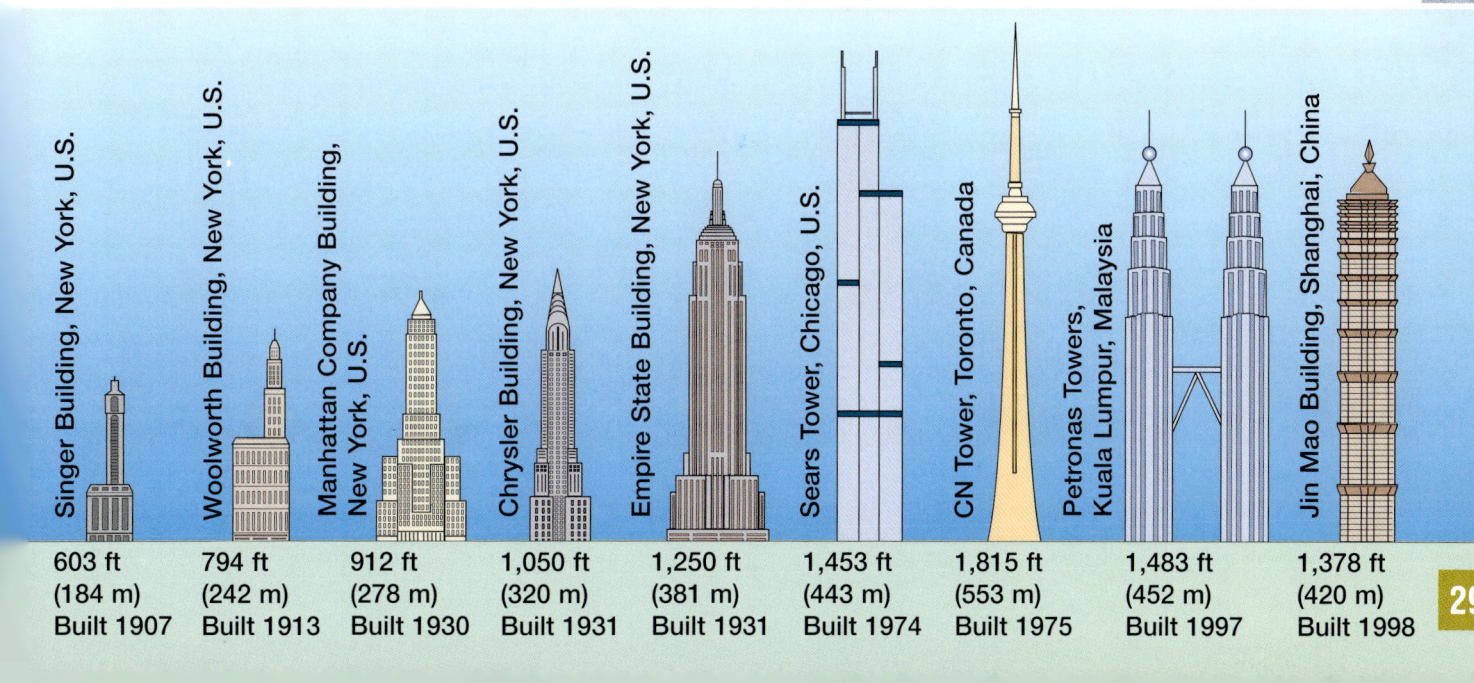

Singer Building, New York, U.S.	Woolworth Building, New York, U.S.	Manhattan Company Building, New York, U.S.	Chrysler Building, New York, U.S.	Empire State Building, New York, U.S.	Sears Tower, Chicago, U.S.	CN Tower, Toronto, Canada	Petronas Towers, Kuala Lumpur, Malaysia	Jin Mao Building, Shanghai, China
603 ft (184 m) Built 1907	794 ft (242 m) Built 1913	912 ft (278 m) Built 1930	1,050 ft (320 m) Built 1931	1,250 ft (381 m) Built 1931	1,453 ft (443 m) Built 1974	1,815 ft (553 m) Built 1975	1,483 ft (452 m) Built 1997	1,378 ft (420 m) Built 1998

USING MODELS TO LEARN ABOUT STRUCTURES

You can find out about some of the challenges engineers meet when they design and build a skyscraper or tower by using a construction set to build your own. Construction sets have the same parts as skyscrapers and towers. They have members that can be joined or screwed together to make a frame, bases that act as foundations, and cladding materials, too.

Strength and stability are just as important in a construction set as they are in a life-sized structure. Many of today's engineers and architects started with construction sets. They are still building with them—the construction sets just grew bigger.

▲ Construction sets are a great way to learn about strong and stable skyscrapers and towers.

GLOSSARY

architects	people who design buildings
ball bearing	a metal ball placed between two things to allow them to move smoothly against each other
brace	something fastened to an object to keep it stiff and straight, just like the braces worn on teeth
cement	an ingredient in concrete which makes the concrete harden like stone
concrete	a building material made by mixing cement and sand or gravel with water
corkscrew	spiral-shaped or spinning like a spiral
engineers	people who design and build large structures
excavators	people or machines that dig
flexible	able to bend without breaking
fog	a thick mist of water droplets that hangs in the air
foundations	a firm base upon which a structure is built
geologists	scientists who study rocks and soil
hoists	machines specially made for lifting very heavy things
horizontal	level or flat
materials	anything used to make a structure
piles	concrete or metal poles buried in the ground
reinforced	made stronger
rivets	pins which are used to fasten sheets of metal together
stable	something that will not wobble or fall
structure	something that is made up of many parts joined together
temporary	for a short time only
vertical	standing upright
welded	two pieces of metal joined together by heating their ends until they melt into one
wind tunnel	a specially built tunnel where fans are used to move the air at different speeds

INDEX

A
accidents 25, 26–27
air-conditioning 25
aircraft 27

B
Bank of China Building 11
beams 11, 22
braced-frame skyscrapers 5, 13
building materials 4, 10–11, 12

C
cables 15, 18
Canada National Tower 5, 29
Centrepoint Tower 15
Citicorp Center 24, 26
cladding 8, 11, 23, 25
columns 11, 22, 24
concrete 11, 18, 21, 22
concrete-core skyscrapers 5, 14, 22
cranes 19

D
design 5, 6–7, 8–9, 12–15, 16, 26–27, 30

E
earthquakes 8, 13, 16, 24, 26
Eiffel Tower 5, 10, 15
electricity towers 15
elevators 20, 22, 25
Empire State Building 10, 20, 27

F
fire 27
Flat Iron Building 5
floors 11, 23
foundations 8, 17–18
frame 8, 13–14, 19, 20, 21

G
guyed towers 15

I
iron 10

J
Jenney, William Le Baron 20
John Hancock Center 12, 25

L
Leaning Tower of Pisa 18
lighthouses 28

M
maintenance 25
member 11
models 30

O
oil rigs 28

P
Petronas Towers 12, 29
piles 17
pyramids 5, 7, 16

R
rectangles 6–7, 16
reinforced concrete 11, 21
rigid-frame skyscrapers 5, 13

S
San Francisco Airport 24
Sears Tower 12, 21
shot towers 28
slab 18
steel 10, 11
steel-framed concrete core skyscrapers 5, 14
steel-framed tube skyscrapers 5, 14, 21
stone 10, 20
structures 4, 6

T
termites 4, 22
towers 15, 28, 29
Trans-America Building 16
triangles 6–7
tuned mass damper 24

W
walls 23
watch tower 28
wind 9, 12, 13, 21, 24, 26
World Trade Center 27